The Wee Book of

Shirley McKay

Black & White Publishing

First published 2004

by Black & White Publishing Ltd

99 Giles Street, Edinburgh EH6 6BZ

ISBN 1 84502 032 4

A CIP catalogue record for this book is available from The British Library.

Printed and bound in Spain by Bookprint, S.L., Barcelona.

INTRODUCTION

According to legend, the first Pictish king of Alba – a name for early Scotland – divided up his land into seven kingdoms and named them after his seven sons. Today, only one, the one he called *Fib*, survives intact. With the North Sea to the east, the Firth of Forth to the south and the Firth of Tay to the north acting as fixed boundaries, *Fib* became the Kingdom of Fife. Over the years, however, its border to the west has proved rather more fluid than the other three.

The region's geography has shaped and continues to shape the lives of the people who live here. Central Fife, especially the area around the River Eden, is known as the 'Howe'. This is fertile farmland that gently rises to meet the Lomond Hills. In the coastal towns and villages of the East Neuk – *neuk* is Scots for 'corner' – fishing was the primary source of income for many and the influence of early trade with continental Europe, especially the Low Countries, is clear to see. With their distinctive crow-stepped gable roofs and terracotta pantiles, the houses in villages such as Culross have a character that is entirely their own, often seeming as though they have been preserved in some remote era of the past.

Having said that, many of the ways of life depicted in this little book have now disappeared completely. Kirkcaldy's linoleum factories have either been pulled down or converted into flats and community centres – some would say this is no bad thing as the 'queer-like' smell that emanated from them was pretty disgusting. The linen looms and flax fields are all gone and few can even explain how the old salt pans used to work. Over the last fifty years, the output of Fife's coal mines has gradually declined and the once-teeming harbours have seen their fleets reduced from hundreds of vessels to just a few.

On the plus side, however, the Fife tourist trade is booming like never before. The Kingdom's picturesque villages, sandy beaches, historic towns and, of course, its golf all continue to attract visitors from near and far.

Pushing relentlessly onwards to Fife. the Romans were the first to build a transitory boat-bridge as a means of crossing the Forth. Medieval pilgrims were transported across the River Forth to the Kingdom of Fife aboard the Queen's Ferry, which gave its name to communities on both sides of the firth. The ferry would have had unpredictable tides to contend with. It was not until the early 1800s, when the landing piers were built, that the journey into Fife became less arduous.

The construction of the Forth Rail Bridge in 1890 eased the passage further but boats continued to cross the Forth until just after the opening of the Forth Road Bridge in 1964. Here, a 1950s ferry makes her way towards Fife with the famous rail bridge in the background. On the last of these ferries, a traveller could convey his goat across the Forth to Fife for five old pence. Today you can transport your family, your car and your goat, if you've got one, across the Forth Road Bridge into Fife for 80p.

Here at Deep Sea World, North Queensferry, these piranha fish seem to be sizing up the prospect of lunch in the shape of a young visitor. In the early 1990s, an abandoned rock quarry beneath the Forth Rail Bridge was flooded to create this vast aquarium – it's a watery zoo of sand tiger sharks, lion fish, stingrays and, the most venomous of all marine life, stonefish. These predators, amphibians and reptiles have their own enclosures, while shoals of sea fish gawk back at those who have come to observe them in the depths that are their home. The aquarium boasts one of the longest underwater walkways in the world and, inside it, 400,000 visitors explore this makeshift ocean fin by jowl each year. The more intrepid of them can join the divers in the tanks and swim with the sharks. The faint of heart need not apply.

This lad had better look out in case he's taken for a spy! He appears to be making notes about these two vessels berthed at the Royal Dockyard, Rosyth. The garden city of Rosyth is built on reclaimed land around the naval base and dockyards that were constructed here in tidal waters in the early 1900s. The fortunes of the people of the southern coast of Fife are inextricably linked with the fate of their dockyard, which, for many years, was the main employer in the region. Here, minesweepers and Polaris submarines would regularly come in for refitting but, at the end of the Cold War, the Ministry of Defence announced the privatisation of the Royal Dockyard and, with it, the loss to the base of the submarine contract. Rosyth was bought by Babcock International in 1997.

The F812 ship in the picture is the Dutch Air Defence Frigate Jacob van Heemskerck.

The Royal Burgh of Culross, (pronounced coo-ross) is twelve miles to the west of the Forth Road Bridge. The little town has been carefully restored by the National Trust in Scotland and has itself become a bridge to the past. The architecture here and in the East Neuk reflects the early influence of foreign trade on Fife's domestic life. The Dutch and Flemish terracotta-coloured pantile roofs, the crow-stepped gable ends and cobbled streets remain much as they were when they were built in the sixteenth and seventeenth centuries. But this peaceful scene belies the history of what was once a bustling seaport. From here, coal, salt and Culross iron were shipped across the seas.

This is a view of the Mercat Cross and Bishop Leighton's Study. The Study's panelled walls are original and date from 1633 and its stunning seventeenth-century painted ceilings have been restored in all their glorious colours. From the tower of the Study, you can look out right across the Forth.

Dunfermline Abbey is believed to be the resting place of nine kings, seven queens, six princes and two princesses. The present ruin dates from the twelfth century, when King David I endowed the Benedictine priory, first established by his mother, Saint Margaret, and guaranteed the fortunes of the church. In this shot, the major structure that you can see on the left of the photo is the south wall of the refectory and it leads towards the gatehouse.

Beyond the gatehouse are the remains of Dunfermline Palace, perching at the top of Pittencrieff Glen and overlooking the beautiful Pittencrief Park, a gift to the city from its most famous son of recent times, Andrew Carnegie. It was in Dunfermline Palace, in 1600, that Anne of Denmark, wife of James VI, gave birth to the future Charles I. His brother Robert, who died in infancy, lies interred within the vaults. The abbey and palace are now cared for by Historic Scotland. Their grounds are home to peacocks who, appropriately, behave as proud as kings but, here too, rabbits frisk about on the grass, undaunted by the presence of their regal neighbours – past or present.

This is the nineteenth-century eastern tower of the Abbey Church of Dunfermline. The so-called 'modern' tower is inscribed with the legend KING ROBERT THE BRUCE, with one word appearing on each of its four sides. During 1817–21, this part was rebuilt from ruins to form the parish church. The gable had fallen in 1726 and little record of the older stone survives. As they were laying the foundations for the new church, the builders came across the bones of King Robert I. After his death, Robert's breastbone had been broken open for the removal of the organs and his heart was taken to the Holy Land. On its return, the heart was buried beneath the Chapter House floor of Melrose Abbey. In 1819, the bones the builders had found were reinterred. King Robert the Bruce had been among the first and foremost kings of Scotland to be buried at Dunfermline and, with the reburial of his bones beneath the pulpit of the new church, he also became the last.

*Here we see Andrew Carnegie, 'Laird of Pittencrieff',
surveying Pittencrieff Glen in Pittencrieff Park. The
philanthropist was born in 1835, the son of a handloom
weaver in the auld grey toun of Dunfermline. Despairing
of work in the steam-driven mills, the family emigrated to
Pittsburgh in 1848, where Andrew rose from bobbin boy
to businessman, forging his fortune in ironworks and steel.
When his company was sold to become US Steel in 1901,
Carnegie became the richest man in the world. He used his
wealth to public good, funding libraries, concert halls and
educational institutions, believing that 'the man who dies
thus rich, dies disgraced'. Returning home, he bought the
'paradise' of Pittencrieff Estate as 'sweet revenge' before
gifting the whole to Dunfermline town. As the child of an
activist family, he had once been forbidden to pass
through the estate grounds.*

This may not be downtown Manhattan but the citizens of Dunfermline are equally proud of their Carnegie Hall, which was opened in the 1930s by the Carnegie Dunfermline Trust. The trust was established in 1903 and its stated aim was 'to bring into the monotonous lives of the toiling masses of Dunfermline more of sweetness and light'. Much emphasis was placed on music and the venue today provides a varying programme of concerts and film, pantomime, comedy, drama and dance.

Carnegie is buried in Sleepy Hollow to the north-west of New York beneath a simple Celtic cross that tells nothing but the hour and place of his birth and death. But the libraries, public baths and music halls that bear his name throughout the world are real and living testament to his philanthropy and his legacies continue to expand.

The Royal Palace of Falkland nestles below the Lomond Hills. It was once the stronghold of the earls of Fife and was rebuilt to serve the Stuart kings as a country home and hunting lodge. Mary Queen of Scots spent her happiest days here as she went hawking in the grounds on her return from France. The building was extensively refashioned in French Renaissance style by her father James V, who built the Royal Tennis Court where real – or royal – tennis continues to be played. In sixteenth-century Scotland, the game was known as 'caitch' and the tennis court as the 'caitchpule'.

When the young James Melville, who would go on to become a great Scottish Presbyterian reformer and educator, arrived at St Andrews to study, he wrote that his father had given him 'glub an bals fur goff but nocht a purse fur catch pull and tavern'. Clearly his father put more emphasis on his son playing golf than he did on him spending time on the tennis courts or in the pub.

This is Auchtermuchty, the setting for the 1992 TV series Dr Finlay, *the STV remake of the 1960s' classic series* Dr Finlay's Casebook. *Auchtermuchty (or Muchty as it is known to its friends) transformed itself into Tannochbrae for the purposes of the TV drama – hence the name of this little café.*

It is a measure of the timelessness of many of Fife's towns that they have often been used as film sets. The Winter Guest *was filmed in Pittenweem and Elie. Culross was the setting for* Kidnapped *and* The Little Vampire. *Memorably, the West Sands of St Andrews played host to* Chariots of Fire *and, more recently,* Stroke of Genius. Macbeth *and* The Bruce *both feature Dunfermline Abbey and* A Shot at Glory *has Crail as its backdrop. Not all of these films have met with critical acclaim but most are welcomed by the locals who appear in them as extras and then eagerly watch the footage, trying to spot themselves.*

Here you can see a shot from the filming of Dr Finlay. *The series featured Jason Flemyng as Dr Neil, Annette Crosbie as the housekeeper Janet Macpherson, David Rintoul as Dr Finlay and the late Ian Bannen as the lovably irascible Dr Cameron. The other star of the drama is Auchtermuchty. The town played the part of Tannochbrae and all that was required for it to give a stunning performance was the addition of a sheep pen, some straw and the odd vintage car.*

The series ran for three years, from 1993 to 1996, and followed the fortunes of an older, slightly jaded Dr Finlay as he worked as a GP in a Scottish country town shortly after the end of the Second World War. Any anachronistically new walls were disguised with rubber bricks and 200 locals, including some children, keenly donned post-war clothes to take part.

This is a statue of the legendary Scottish country dance band leader Jimmy Shand. He proudly stands in his hometown of Auchtermuchty, holding the famous push-button accordion with which he charmed the world. His was the first Scottish dance band to feature in the music charts when 'Bluebell Polka' became a hit in 1955. Jimmy died in December 2000, at the age of ninety-two and, throughout his long career, his music was met with huge acclaim.

The extent of his fame is reflected by the fact that a portrait of him hangs in the National Portrait Gallery of Scotland. He has given his name to trains, streets and pubs and, in 1998, he became Sir James when he received his knighthood from the queen. But here in Auchtermuchty, as in East Wemys where he was born, he is simply Jimmy Shand, fingers poised and always ready to play. The statue's inscription is the so-called Tyler's toast, 'Happy to meet, sorry to part, happy to meet again.'

The ancient craft of bobbin lace-making is kept alive in the Bothy of the Fife Folk Museum in Ceres. Based in the old weigh house on Ceres High Street, the Folk Museum records several hundred years of domestic life and trade in rural Fife. The seventeenth-century tolbooth has been restored with antique weights displayed above and a prisoner languishing below. Adjoining cottages have examples of various craftsmen's art. Cobblers, blacksmiths, miners, tinsmiths, panners for salt, weavers, flax spinners, dressmakers and workers in linen and lace are all represented. Here in the Bothy, farming tools are interspersed with curious mementoes – the patent 'hobby-horse Macmillan bicycle', a doll's house, spectacles said to have belonged to the murdered Archbishop Sharp together with his assassin's boot (was it left Cinderella-style at the scene?), a derelict bus stop – and each has a story to tell.

From his niche on the High Street, the 'last provost of Ceres' squatly surveys the lay of the land. This resolute, fierce little figure is said to represent the Reverend Thomas Buchanan, provost of Ceres from 1578 to 1599. Carved by local stonemason John Howie in the nineteenth century, for almost a hundred years the sculpture remained half-hidden in the wall of the old Ceres manse.

Then, in 1933, it was sold and relocated to Cupar. But local outcry brought the provost home, first to a quiet spot within the churchyard and then, in 1939, to his present alcove on the street. With his tricorn hat and square-set build, the stone provost is often likened to a Toby jug. He now has the air of one who won't be moved again.

This is a view of Scotstarvit Tower, near Cupar. The tower was sold by the Inglis family in 1611 to Sir John Scot, author of the sublimely scornful Scot of Scotstarvit's Staggering State of Scots Statesmen. *Scot endowed the chair of humanity at St Andrews University and was instrumental in publishing the first maps of Scotland, the work of Timothy Pont. A fine example of an L-shaped sixteenth-century tower house, the castle is believed to date in part from 1500, with final alterations made in 1627. A turnpike staircase leads down to a vaulted basement and up to five upper storeys and the ramparts at the top.*

For the keenly satirical Sir John, the naming of his new estate, which had been known as 'Inglis Tarvit' since the thirteenth century, involved a certain satisfaction. He had at last replaced the English with the Scots.

Here you can see Hill of Tarvit House, near Cupar. The present house was designed by Sir Robert Lorimer in 1906 for jute magnate Frederick Sharp, both as a family home and as a showcase for his priceless collection of furniture, tapestries, porcelain, paintings and bronze. Lorimer equipped the house with all the comforts and conveniences of early twentieth-century life. It was one of the first homes in Scotland to benefit from central heating, electric light, telephones, early Shanks lavatory (patented for Lorimer coyly as Remirol, *a reversal of his name), plate-warming cupboards and showers. The last essential of Edwardian country life – the servants – could be summoned by means of a calling system.*

The mansion is now open to public and stands much as the last owners left it. Sharp's daughter died childless in 1948, leaving both the house and its precious contents to The National Trust for Scotland.

*They say a bird in the hand is worth two in the bush
and the bird in question here is a Harris' hawk pictured
at the Scottish Deer Centre, Bow-of-Fife, near Cupar.
The centre is home to nine different species of deer, each
with its own enclosed paddock in fifty-five acres of land.
Visitors can also observe wolves from treetop walkways,
help the rangers feed the deer or watch the breathtaking
flying displays put on by hawks and falcons during the
summer months. The Harris' hawk is popular with
falconers for its affectionate disposition, readiness to
learn and ease of handling. Harris' hawks frequently
become devoted to their handlers – as this one clearly is.*

*Lucky visitors might also glimpse an increasingly rare
sight – a red squirrel. Red squirrels are Scotland's native
squirrel but their grey cousins are gradually invading
their habitat.*

*Here, the crowds are impressed by the Red Arrows'
display at the Leuchars Air Show, as their traditional red,
white and blue jet trails appear in the skies. For one day
in September each year, staff at Leuchars Railway Station
erect barricades to stream the vast influx of visitors into
orderly queues. Commemorating the Battle of Britain, the
annual Leuchars Air Show attracts more than 50,000
spectators and aircraft from all over Europe, including
German Luftwaffe, French naval planes and the full flight
force of the British Royal Air Force, the Royal Navy and
the Army Air Corps. This is the largest show of military
air power in Britain.*

*For the classic aircraft enthusiast, the early Folland Gnat
is also flown. On the ground, there are flight simulations
and static exhibits, funfairs, crafts and market stalls with
aviation themes, while, in the air, the unmissable Utterly
Butterly Barnstormers wing-walking team performs.*

This is St Athernase Church, the parish church of Leuchars and one of the finest examples of Norman architecture in Scotland. Built by Robert de Quinci between 1183 and 1187, the church was dedicated to St Athernase in 1244. The building must have connections with Dunfermline Abbey as some of the same masons' marks are engraved in the stones of both buildings. This suggests that a group of itinerant workers moved around the area plying their trade wherever it was required.

Only the chancel and apse, pictured here on the right, are original. The pepper-pot tower was introduced in 1745, to replace an earlier addition, and the square-box nave replaces one demolished in the nineteenth century. Nonetheless, the ornate blind arcades of the tiered apse and chancel have endured more than eight hundred years of architects, weather and war. St Athernase Church, from its place on the hill, continues to hold its command.

*On the left of this photo is part of the remains of
St Andrews Cathedral and to the right you can see
St Rule's Tower. The ruins dominate the landscape from
the east, rising above the medieval streets of the town
which was formerly known as Kilrimont. There are two
versions of how the relics of St Andrew came to the
town. The more romantic story tells of a fourth-century
Greek monk, called St Rule, who was sailing to Scotland
when he was shipwrecked. Amongst his cargo were the
fingers, kneecap, arm and tooth of St Andrew. The more
probable version is of a bone-collector, named Bishop
Acca of Hexham, hawking his wares to Christian Celts
in 733. But, however and whenever the relics got there,
they were certainly responsible for bringing a stream of
pilgrims in their wake. Kilrimont was renamed St
Andrews and the town became the ecclesiastical centre
of Scotland. The massive cathedral, begun in 1160, was
finally consecrated in 1318, in the presence of Robert
the Bruce. Fire and storm, war, wind and Reformation
all played their part in its eventual dereliction.*

This is St Andrews Castle. The medieval bishops and archbishops of St Andrews required a residence that reflected their status as leaders of the Church of Scotland and offered protection in turbulent times. Their castle was built on the cliff to the north of the town. Nothing is left of the earliest buildings – what survives now dates back to the fourteenth century, when Bishop Trail rebuilt the walls of a castle that had been garrisoned and under siege many times. In the 1540s, during a lengthy siege of the castle by Protestant lairds, a mine was dug by would-be invaders. The castle's occupants, who included the Protestant reformer John Knox, dug a countermine and successfully repelled them – but not for long. Eventually, the besiegers triumphed and Knox was taken prisoner and sent to France to work as a galley slave.

The two mines were discovered during excavations in the nineteenth century and they reveal just how ingenious sixteenth-century warfare was. And the castle's notorious bottle dungeon is testament to the severity of the era's cruelties. This was indeed a bloody place where, according to John Knox, 'many of God's children were imprisoned'. Shortly after that mid-sixteenth-century siege, the bishops left and the once-proud castle gradually fell into a state of disrepair.

The extensive sandy beaches at St Andrews offer hours of fun and relaxation. This is a view of the East Sands and, in June 2004, it joined St Andrews West Sands in receiving a coveted European Blue Flag, meaning that it meets all the standards expected in terms of cleanliness, safety and being well managed. Of the six Scottish Blue Flag beaches, five are located in Fife. (The other three are Elie Harbour, Burntisland and Aberdour Silver Sands.) For those visitors who come here to the caravans at Kinkell Braes, many from the west of Scotland, the award given to St Andrews East Sands will come as no surprise. Curving round between the harbour and the cliffs, the bay is ideal for windsurfing and yachts. It is also home to a sailing club and, for the (occasional?) rainy day, there's a swimming pool in the nearby leisure centre.

During university term time, after Sunday morning chapel, a few (fool)hardy or hung-over students still attempt the 'pier walk', red gowns flapping fiercely in the wind.

Overlooking St Andrews Old Course is the Old Course Hotel. Those approaching St Andrews from the east will see the harbour and the ruined cathedral and castle. On a clear day, the shoreline will be sparkling and they'll be able to look right across the water to Dundee. But nowadays most people come here from the west and for many, the reason for coming to St Andrews is not to visit a holy place, but a different pilgrimage of an altogether different nature. From their perspective, the town is defined by the golf courses rising from the West Sands. The gatehouse for them is the Old Course Hotel. Built in 1968, over 200 years after the Old Course was established, the hotel overlooks both the Royal and Ancient Clubhouse and the infamous seventeenth Road Hole which takes its name from the much-feared Road Bunker. This hazard has been the undoing of many a golfer hoping to make par on what is generally thought of as the world's most famous golf hole.

This is the eighteenth hole of the Old Course, St Andrews. On a website dedicated to Scottish golf courses, this one is described as being designed by Mother Nature and Old Tom Morris. Behind the green is the Royal and Ancient Clubhouse. The Royal and Ancient Golf Club oversees the rules of golf in over 100 affiliated nations. In the summer of 2004, the club celebrated its 250th anniversary with a series of dinners held in the largest marquee ever seen in St Andrews, seating 1,200 people. The club began more modestly, though hardly less exclusively, as the Society of St Andrews Golfers founded by twenty-two 'noblemen and gentlemen' to preserve the reputation of St Andrews as the true 'alma mater of the golf'. The early members had no clubhouse. Meeting in 1766 once a fortnight to 'play around the links', each paid a shilling for his dinner 'the absent as well as the present'. This suggests that not all of the twenty-two turned up for what they had termed as the 'healthful exercise of golf' and this rule of paying for dinner, whether it was eaten or not, ensured a guaranteed sum each fortnight.

Appropriately situated in St Andrews, the home of golf, the British Golf Museum is within striking distance of the Royal and Ancient clubhouse. It chronicles the history of golf from its beginnings in the middle ages until the present day. Its long associations with a town already in the 1690s recognised as the 'metropolis of golfing' are played out in full, from Mary Queen of Scots' diversions on the links to Tiger Woods' triumph in the 2000 Open. An eclectic collection of artefacts and memorabilia extends from the poignant 'lark killed by a golf ball' to the eccentric golfing toilet seat.

Younger visitors are welcome to try out the antique clubs and balls and nineteenth-century clothes in the museum's newest gallery which is called The Eighteenth Hole. There is also a mini putting green where you can experiment with different types of ball. Discover which runs truer – an old gutta-percha, one stuffed with feathers or one with a rubber core.

Founded in 1410, when a papal bull issued by Pope Benedict XIII granted it university status, St Andrews is Scotland's oldest university. This is a shot of the quadrangle of the university's St Mary's College. Archbishop Beaton founded the college in 1539 and at that time it was called the New College. When the first students entered the college, its main emphasis was the same as that of its continental cousins – the teaching of ancient texts. But, following the Reformation, the college became the university's Theological Faculty and, since then, it has continued to teach religion. It is now the Faculty and School of Divinity.

Despite the changes over the years, the quadrangle in this picture looks much the same as it must have done when the college first opened its doors. The quadrangle is a pleasant leafy place with a holm oak, thought to be about 250 years old, and a thorn tree that is said to have been planted by Mary Queen of Scots.

This is 'Raisin Monday' at the University of St Andrews, the culmination of a weekend's heavy drinking in November. The celebrations stem from the custom of the more senior students 'adopting' first-year students – known as bejants and bejantines – to help ease them into the rigours of scholarly life. These 'academic parents' are rewarded with gifts of raisins – generally preferred in liquid form. In return, they issue a Raisin Receipt written in Latin. It was originally written on parchment but now they try to find the most cumbersome things they can for the bejants and bejantines to carry through the town – shop signs, people, even cars.

For the first-years, drinking begins on the Sunday and continues until eleven the next morning. The event ends here in St Salvator's Quad, where they are expected to exhibit their receipts. By this time, many of them are in fancy dress – often wearing baby clothes to reflect their inexperienced status. It all finishes with a free-for-all foam fight. Shopkeepers stock up on shaving foam and try their best to make sure their trolleys aren't taken away to be used as receipts.

Here, His Royal Highness Prince William of Wales is strolling by St Salvator's Chapel, St Andrews. In September 2001, the University of St Andrews welcomed among its intake of first year undergraduates the queen's grandson, Prince William, second in line to the throne. William chose St Andrews over Edinburgh because he felt that the town had a 'real community feel to it', a sentiment he echoed at the end of his second year. He was, he claimed, a 'country boy at heart'. Embarking on a four-year arts degree in the traditional Scottish system, he soon became a familiar face about the town, grateful to the locals who 'very kindly' went quietly on with their lives.

The admissions office, always busy, now bows beneath the weight of applications – an unprecedented number of them from North American females hoping to catch the eye of the prince.

*Without a word, Bob Dylan accepted his honorary
doctorate from the University of St Andrews on 24 June
2004 before making his escape in this car. The last time
he accepted such a degree was at Princeton in 1970. This
was the blazing hot day he recalls in 'The Day of the
Locusts'. Two of the lines from that song are:*

> There was little to say, no conversation,
> As I stepped to the stage to pick up my degree

*and, with them, the precedent of no thank-you speech
was set.*

*Whatever this college dropout's feelings towards the
academic world are now, he chose to take his doctorate of
music, at the age of sixty-three, from the poets and
professors of St Andrews. In complete contrast to that hot
day in 1970, Dr Zimmerman had to brave savage winds
and driving rain that were more typical of winter than
late June. When he left, with never a word and the car
windows blacked out, it was scarcely any clearer who had
been honouring whom.*

This is a 1960s shot of Kirkcaldy's famous Links Market. Stretching over a distance of nearly a mile, it is thought to be Europe's longest street fair. The market was started in medieval times when it was held as a weekly trading market for farmers and craftsmen. In 1304, it was granted a royal charter, mainly as a means of collecting taxes. Since then, a fair, lasting for a week around Easter, has been held on Kirkcaldy's Esplanade each year. Even in its earliest days there are records of street entertainers such as acrobats and jugglers and they evolved into the showmen of the nineteenth century. Victorians would wonder at exotic performing animals and be shocked by the so-called 'freaks', which included anything from bearded ladies to dwarfs and people with unusual deformities. The men would hope to impress the ladies with their displays of skill and strength.

At the time this photo was taken, fair-goers could enjoy the 'sensational thrill' of the waltzer or try their luck at 'Jimmy's Bingo'. The kids could have a go on the 'Golden Galloping' carousel and the ice-cream van and candyfloss stall provided treats for all.

Kirkcaldy, called The Lang Toun because its buildings stretch for such a distance along the coast, became the centre of floorcloth manufacture when Michael Nairn built his first canvas factory. Known locally as 'Nairn's folly', it looked down on the town from high upon the cliffs at Pathhead sands. Folly or not, by 1874 five other floorcloth factories had opened and, with the introduction of linoleum in 1877, many local people were employed in the new industry. The linoleum was made from a solidified mixture of linseed oil and ground cork backed on canvas, hand-coloured and printed with blocks. Affordable and easy to clean, it brought about a minor revolution in domestic life. The lino printers worked in pairs, hand-stamping painted blocks on to the floor to form the pattern. Each printer had a 'tier-boy' apprentice, whose job it was to 'tier' or spread the paint.

The boiling vats of linseed oil produced the 'distinctive' smell that is referred to in the poem 'The Boy on the Train':

> I'll sune be ringin' ma Gran'ma's bell,
> She'll cry, 'Come ben, my laddie.'
> For I ken mysel, by the queer-like smell,
> That the next stop's Kirkcaddy!

This is Methil Docks in 1964. The dockyards were established in the 1870s for the transportation of Fife coal across the Forth. By 1913, three docks had been constructed, the third built to accommodate up to eight hydraulic coal hoists, and Methil became the main coal port in Scotland. But, by the time this photograph was taken, the collieries of Fife were already beginning to decline. In 1977, the massive third dock ceased operation, with any last exports being channelled through Leith.

In 1998, East Fife Football Club moved to their brand new stadium, New Bayview, at Methil Docks and waterfront office blocks now stand on parts of the site. Although the whole area of the former dockyards had been earmarked for development in 1996, sadly, the proposed marina, sailing club and exclusive leisure zones remain a distant dream.

On Main Street, Lower Largo, the statue of a man in goatskins marks the place where a thatched cottage once stood. This was the birthplace of Alexander Selkirk. Born in 1676, Selkirk is the supposed inspiration behind Daniel Defoe's famous castaway Robinson Crusoe. The seventh son of a Largo shoemaker, he was a wayward youth and, in 1695, having apparently behaved indecently in church, he was due to stand before the Kirk Session to be reprimanded. Instead, he ran away to sea.

In September 1704, after quarrelling with his captain, he was abandoned, at his own request, on the uninhabited South Pacific island of Juan Fernandez, to take his chance with the next passing ship. Over four years later, in February 1709, he was found and was soon made mate of the privateer that had rescued him. Later he was given his own ship to command and, in 1712, to the surprise of his family who had presumed him long dead, he returned to his hometown a very wealthy man. Selkirk couldn't settle back into normal life and lived in isolation in his home area for many years, sometimes in a cave. He joined the navy in 1720 and died at sea, probably of yellow fever, in 1723, by which time he had attained the rank of lieutenant.

The lighthouse seen here amongst these dangerous rocky outcrops is Elie Ness. It was built by the Stevenson family in 1908 and remains an active aid to navigation today – its white flashing light breaks through the darkness every six seconds and is visible for eighteen nautical miles. Earlsferry, situated on the other side of Elie Bay, closed as a port in 1766. This was because the whole harbour flooded when storm-shifted sands swamped it. Seven men drowned in the catastrophe. In the Scottish Fisheries Museum at Anstruther, there is a quiet corner dedicated to all the Scots fishermen who lost their lives at sea.

The start of one of Fife's Millennium Cycleways is at Elie Harbour. The nineteen-mile on- and off-road route takes cyclists on a loop that passes close to The Peat Inn, a restaurant and inn that is a firm favourite with locals and tourists alike. A bowl of the famous Peat Inn Smoked Fish Soup is just what a weary cyclist needs before getting back in the saddle.

Along the coastal path from Elie to St Monans an eighteenth-century folly stands on the rocks looking out to sea. This is Lady's Tower and it was built by Sir John Anstruther of Elie House as a summerhouse for his wife Janet Fall. The tower lies close to Ruby Bay, which takes its name from the fact that garnets – also called Elie rubies – have been found on its beach. The bay is where Janet liked to bathe – naked. A stunning beauty, she used the tower as her changing room and left her clothes there as she dipped among the waves. While she was in the water, a bellman is reputed to have walked through the town to warn – or perhaps to tantalise – the locals that she was swimming. She had a reputation as a flirt.

Today, the ruin provides a scenic resting-place or picnic spot for those who make their way along the sands – but few are as brave as the fair Janet and take to the icy waves.

This is St Monan's Windmill and it is almost all that remains of the area's once thriving salt industry. On the shore in front of the windmill are the vestiges of several salt-pan houses. Sea water would have been drawn up on to metal beds or pans, probably using power from the windmill. Below the pans, coal fires raged night and day, boiling off the water. It took three boiling sessions, using between six and eight tons of coal, to obtain one ton of salt and egg white or bulls' blood were used to extract any impurities.

Because the fires required round-the-clock attention, workers' cottages were sited right next to the salt-pan houses and often whole families were involved in the business. Women and children were employed in hauling coal for the fires and in taking the salt away to be dried.

The abundance of easily quarried coal nearby meant this was an ideal place for the industry and, behind the windmill at Coal Farm, crop marks indicate where the pitheads once were. The area has been designated as a Site of Special Scientific Interest.

This atmospheric shot shows the Auld Kirk of St Monan's Church in winter. The church sits on the brink of the Forth and is said to be the 'closest to the sea' of all the kirks in Scotland.

The site is believed to be where a shrine to St Monan was erected. In the days before heating, the church's exposed position meant that Sunday worship must have been a bit of an endurance test – reports testify to it being a cold damp place with the walls covered in green mould. The fact that it still exists is quite amazing as, over its 700-plus years, it has had more than bad weather to contend with. The English burnt it down in 1544 and it was rebuilt in 1646. It was then allowed to fall into a ruinous state and, by 1722, little of the roof remained. In 1825, the Presbytery decreed that it should be pulled down but this was overturned and repair work started in 1828.

What you can see today is a complete restoration to its former Gothic glory. In the 1950s, a sister of one of the kirk's long-serving ministers, the Rev. Turnbull, left money for this purpose in her will. The church was closed for about four years while the restorative work went on and it was rededicated in 1961. Its dramatic location and imposing aspect make it a very popular choice for weddings.

In this shot we are looking up one of Pittenweem's steep braes towards the entrance to St Fillan's Cave. Legend has it that, in the seventh century, St Fillan came here to teach the gospels and made this cave his home. He was known as a great scholar and writer of sermons, often studying and writing day and night. The legend goes on to say that, when asked how he managed this in the darkness of his cave, he said that God illuminated his arm.

In the thirteenth century, monks built a priory on the hill above St Fillan's cave and used the cool cave as a kind of natural refrigerator for storing their grain and other perishables. By the eighteenth century, St Fillan's Cave had been put to yet another purpose when it became a place for smugglers and thieves to stash their goods and sometimes even hide themselves. During the following century, this holy place suffered the ignominy of being used as the town's rubbish dump but, in the 1930s, all the rubbish was cleared out and a shrine to the saint with the glowing arm was built. It has been a place of pilgrimage ever since and an ecumenical Easter service takes place there each year.

Here, we are looking down on the foreshore and harbour of Pittenweem, where the Fife fishing fleet is based. At Pittenweem Harbour, an impressive new fish market, built in 1994, supplies local shops and restaurants with their daily catch of white fish and prawns. The settlement of Pittenweem dates back to the early seventh century and takes its name from pit *meaning 'place' and* weem *meaning 'cave', the cave being that of St Fillan. The town's religious associations date back to this seventh-century saint and continued with the Benedictine monks who fled here from marauders on the Isle of May. In the sixteenth century, the town became notorious for its zealous pursuit of local witches. The practice lasted until 1705, when the last accused 'Pittenweem witch' was put to death.*

Today it has a more congenial reputation as a community of artists, showcased in the Pittenweem Arts Festival. During the first week of August each year, venues throughout the little town, from the smallest living room to garden sheds and galleries, are opened up to visitors.

The village of Kilconquhar lies just to the north of Elie and here we can see curlers on Kilconquhar Loch with the Gothic-style parish church in the background. The village name looks like it should be pronounced as 'kill-kon-kwar' but bizarrely, as the old Kinneucher Inn on Main Street suggests, Kilconquhar actually rhymes with Leuchars but without the S – kin-oo-kar or kin-oo-char with the <ch> pronounced like that of loch.

Curling on the loch is still practised when the waters freeze and the game represents another link between the East Neuk and the Netherlands – the so-called 'roaring game' was also played on Dutch canals.

In warmer months, the waters here are home to mallard, teal and swans. But the loch's waters also have a more sinister past for it was in Kilconquhar Loch that those found guilty at the witch trials of Pittenweem were drowned.

This 1937 photo of Anstruther – known locally as 'Anster' – harbour shows what a busy place this once was. At that time, it was home to the largest fishing fleet in the East Neuk and, as you can see, it would have been possible to cross the harbour bay by stepping from boat to boat. Today, with the decline of winter herring, only a handful of fishermen trawl for white fish and prawns from here. The harbour is now undergoing redevelopment as a marina for pleasure boats and, during the summer months, the May Princess ferries sightseers back and forth to the Isle of May.

The lifeboat station at Anstruther has a very impressive rescue record. Since the first boat was called on in 1865, there have been 425 launches and 250 lives saved up to 2001. Appropriately, the station's main vessel is the RNLI Kingdom of Fife and, together with her sister boats from North Berwick, Dunbar, South Queensferry and Kinghorn, she operates in the waters of the Firth of Forth and the nearby parts of the North Sea.

This is the courtyard that forms part of the Scottish Fisheries Museum in Anstruther. Housed in a series of historic buildings that include a former boatyard, tavern and cooperage, the museum chronicles the history of boats from barks and rafts to the Zulus, Scaffies and Fifies, from whalers to steam-driven drifters and from various types of engines to curious fish-finding tools. Unless she is out on excursion, the museum's flagship Reaper *berths in the harbour outside. Eleven other full-sized vessels are on display in the boathouse.*

More poignant, though, are the displays of fishermen's possessions, their personal stories and the accounts of loved ones left behind. There is also a cooperage showing barrel production and a reconstruction of herring wives working their fingers raw as they each gutted up to sixty herring a minute. And the interior of a nineteenth-century fisherman's cottage allows visitors an insight into what life was like onshore.

Just three boats are berthed in Anstruther Harbour in this shot where, in days gone by, hundreds would have been jostling for a place. The Anstruther Fish Restaurant, pictured here on Shore Street, before its expansion to include the Fish Bar takeaway, has twice been voted the best in the country and still attracts impressive queues as the shutters start to rise. The local speciality is Pittenweem haddock, freshly caught daily and prepared down the coast at St Monan's. You can have it crisply breadcrumbed or lightly battered and each fish is fried while you wait. It is difficult to beat this for simplicity – the chips are almost incidental – but, for those who still insist on pushing out the boat, they also serve halibut, black-buttered skate and the finest red lobster which they get from Crail.

This 1979 shot shows some of the last of the Anster fisherlassies, gutting and filleting fish near Anstruther shore. To ensure maximum freshness, the fish were processed close to the boats as quickly as possible – to reach the gold standard, they had to be ready for sale within twenty-four hours. These are the last in a long line of Anstruther women who would wait for the catches to come in. For every fisherman who put out to sea, some four or five folk, mainly women and girls, were employed on the land, cleaning and salting the fish, mending nets, baiting lines and taking the fish to the markets for sale.

Film footage from the 1950s, collected by Crail film-maker Mike Hildrey in 2001, shows the fisherlassies and sea queens or quines baiting lines and salting herring – and, despite the smiles on their faces, every one of them had hands that were ragged and red raw.

Deep in the countryside, among the fields of cows, hides 'Scotland's best kept secret'. This is a photo taken inside Scotland's Secret Bunker near Crail. Built in the 1950s, more than forty metres below ground and with a three-metre-thick concrete outer shell, the bunker was where the government and military commanders would have run the country from if there had been a nuclear war. But, with the end of the Cold War, the nuclear threat diminished and the bunker is now a tourist attraction.

Visitors pass through an unassuming farmhouse into dim, dank tunnels where all around the sirens rise and fall. Filing past telephones that look like they could still bring the chilling message that the country is on the brink of nuclear war, they can then see the six dormitories where up to 300 personnel took turns to sleep in six-hour shifts, swapping beds with the next batch in a system called 'hot-bedding'. The operations rooms with what was once state-of-the-art technology now look decidedly amateurish – as does the BBC radio station which would have had to broadcast information and advice should the unthinkable ever have happened. At the end of the tour, visitors are rewarded with cups of tea and Tunnock's teacakes in the bunker's old canteen where, eerily, a jukebox plays the hits of the time.

This is Crail Harbour at low tide. The oldest of the East Neuk burghs, Crail acquired royal status from King David I in the mid twelfth century. In 1310, Robert the Bruce conferred the right to Sunday trading on the Marketgate, which, at the time, was one of the largest medieval markets in Europe. Extensive trade links with the Low Countries have influenced the architecture of the older buildings. Corbie-stepped roofs with their distinctive pantiles are visible throughout the town. The harbour has remained perhaps the most picturesque in the East Neuk and is reproduced on chocolate boxes, jigsaw scenes, tablemats and the like throughout the world. There is even a scale replica constructed of Lego bricks at Legoland in Denmark – complete with harbourmaster's dog. Nonetheless, Crail remains an active harbour, fishing on a small scale for lobster and partan, the famous Crail crab, both of which are sold here from the little hut above the harbour wall.

Here, puffins are nesting on the Isle of May. Lying six miles off the East Neuk shore in the Firth of Forth, the tiny Isle of May has been a nature reserve since 1956. As well as the puffins, there are thousands of breeding pairs of guillemots, kittiwakes, razorbills and shags, creating vast cities of seabirds all vying for enough space to bring up their young. So common are the sea birds that the island's rabbits have begun to evolve, turning camouflage-white in order to blend in with the gulls.

Visitors to the Isle of May will see the remains of a twelfth-century monastery, one of Scotland's first lighthouses, which was built there in 1636, another lighthouse that dates from 1844 and, if they are lucky, colonies of grey seals.